Piano • Vocal • Guitar

THE BEST OF ERIC CLAPTON

Hal Leonard Publishing Corporation

· 7777 West Bluemound Road P.O. Box 13819 Milwaukee, WI 53213

ISBN 0-7935-2388-5

AFTER MIDNIGHT

Words and Music by
JOHN J. CALE

Af - ter mid - night,___ we're gon - na let it all___ hang
Af - ter mid - night,___ we're gon - na shake your tam - bou -

down._____ Af - ter
rine._____ Af - ter

mid - night,__ we're gon - na chug - a - lug__ and shout._____
mid - night,__ it's all gon - na be peach - es__ and cream._____

____ We're gon - na stim - u - late__ some
____ We're gon - na cause talk and__ sus -

ac - tion;__ we're gon - na get some sat - is - fac - tion. We're gon - na find out
pi - cion;__ we're gon - na give an ex - hi - bi - tion. We're gon - na find out

what it is all a - bout._____
what it is all a - bout._____

4

FOREVER MAN

Words and Music by
JERRY LYNN WILLIAMS

BEFORE YOU ACCUSE ME

Words and Music by
EUGENE McDANIELS

CAN'T FIND MY WAY HOME

Words and Music by
STEVE WINWOOD

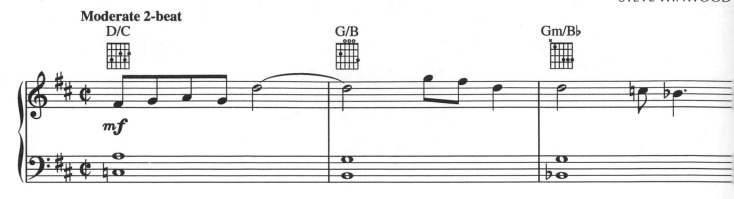

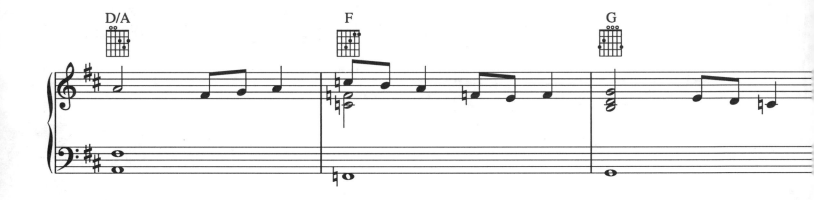

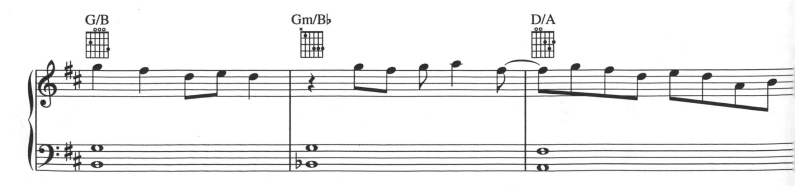

Ooh, _____

COCAINE

Words and Music by
JOHN J. CALE

CROSSROADS

Words and Music by
ROBERT JOHNSON

2. I went down to the crossroad, tried to flag a ride.
   Down to the crossroad, tried to flag a ride.
   Nobody seemed to know me. Everybody passed me by.

3. When I'm goin' down to Rosedale, take my rider by my side.
   Goin' down to Rosedale, take my rider by my side.
   We can still barrelhouse, baby, on the riverside.

4. You can run, you can run. Tell my friend, boy, Willie Brown.
   Run, you can run. Tell my friend, boy, Willie Brown.
   And I'm standin' at the crossroad. Believe I'm sinkin' down.

DO WHAT YOU LIKE

Words and Music by
GINGER BAKER

FOR YOUR LOVE

Words and Music by
GRAHAM GOULDMAN

HAVE YOU EVER LOVED A WOMAN

Words and Music by
BILLY MYLES

2. But you just love that woman so much, it's a shame and a sin.
   You just love that woman so much, it's a shame and a sin.
   But all the time, you know she belongs to your very best friend.

3. Have you ever loved a woman, oh, you know you can't leave her alone?
   Have you ever loved a woman, yes, you know you can't leave her alone?
   Something deep inside of you won't let you wreck your best friend's home.

HELLO OLD FRIEND

Words and Music by
ERIC CLAPTON

I CAN'T STAND IT

Words and Music by
ERIC CLAPTON

I SHOT THE SHERIFF

Words and Music by
BOB MARLEY

2. I shot the sheriff, but I swear it was in self-defense.
   I shot the sheriff, and they say it is a capital offense.
   Sheriff John Brown always hated me; for what, I don't know.
   Every time that I plant a seed, he said, "Kill it before it grows."
   He said, "Kill it before it grows." But I say:

3. I shot the sheriff, but I swear it was in self-defense.
   I shot the sheriff, but I swear it was in self-defense.
   Freedom came my way one day, and I started out of town.
   All of a sudden, I see sheriff John Brown aiming to shoot me down.
   So I shot, I shot him down. But I say:

4. I shot the sheriff, but I did not shoot the deputy.
   I shot the sheriff, but I didn't shoot the deputy.
   Reflexes got the better of me, and what is to be must be.
   Every day, the bucket goes to the well, but one day the bottom will drop out.
   Yes, one day the bottom will drop out. But I say:

I'VE GOT A ROCK 'N' ROLL HEART

Words and Music by TROY SEALS,
EDDIE SETSER and STEVE DIAMOND

43

IT'S IN THE WAY THAT YOU USE IT

Words and Music by ERIC CLAPTON
and ROBBIE ROBERTSON

LAYLA

Words and Music by ERIC CLAPTON
and JIM GORDON

LAY DOWN SALLY

Words and Music by ERIC CLAPTON,
MARCY LEVY and GEORGE TERRY

The talk to you.
I

D. S. %% al Coda ⊕

Coda ⊕

talk to you. __

Repeat and fade

Repeat and fade

LET IT GROW

Words and Music by
ERIC CLAPTON

Repeat
and fade

LOVIN' YOU, LOVIN' ME

Words and Music by ERIC CLAPTON
and BONNIE BRAMLETT

64

NOBODY KNOWS YOU WHEN YOU'RE DOWN AND OUT

Words and Music by
JIMMIE COX

PROMISES

Words and Music by RICHARD FELDMAN
and ROGER LINN

RUNNING ON FAITH

Words and Music by
JERRY WILLIAMS

Late-ly, I've been run-nin' on _____ faith. _____
Late-ly, I've been talk - in' in ___ my sleep.

SEA OF JOY

Words and Music by
STEVE WINWOOD

84

To Coda ⊕

Wait-ing in our boats to set sail,

Sea of Joy.

Sea of

SIGNE

By ERIC CLAPTON

Moderately fast Bossa Nova feel

STRANGE BREW

Words and Music by ERIC CLAPTON,
FELIX PAPPALARDI and GAIL COLLINS

THE SUNSHINE OF YOUR LOVE

Words and Music by JACK BRUCE,
PETE BROWN and ERIC CLAPTON

TEARS IN HEAVEN
(FROM THE MOTION PICTURE "RUSH")

Words and Music by ERIC CLAPTON
and WILL JENNINGS

Would you know my name _____
Would you hold my hand _____
Would you know my name _____

if I saw you in heav-en?
if I I saw you in heav-en?
if I I saw you in heav-en?

Would it be the same _____
Would you help me stand _____
Would you be the same _____

Be - yond the door ___ there's peace, I'm sure. ___

TULSA TIME

Words and Music by
DANNY FLOWERS

Moderate Boogie beat

I ___ left O-kla-ho-ma driv - in' in a Pon-ti-ac
there I was in Hol-ly-wood wish - in' I was do-in' good,

just a-bout to lose ___ my mind, ___ I was
talk-in' on the tel-e-phone line, ___ But they don't

goin' to Ar-i-zo-na, may-be on to Cal-i-for-nia, where the
need me in the mov-ies and no-bod-y sings my songs,

101

born to just walk ___ the line. ___
went on back to Tul - sa time. ___

Liv - in' on Tul - sa time. ___
Liv - in' on Tul - sa time. ___

Liv - in' on Tul - sa time. ___
Liv - in' on Tul - sa time. ___

Well, you know I been thru it when I set my watch back to it,
Gon - na set my watch back to it, cause you know I've been thru it,

1 F

2 F

D.S. and Fade

Liv - in' on ___ Tul - sa time. ___

Well, ___

WHITE ROOM

Words and Music by JACK BRUCE
and PETE BROWN

Moderately, with a beat

In a white room with black
no strings could se-

cur - tains near the sta - tion.
cure you at the sta - tion.

Black - roof
Plat - form

WILLIE AND THE HAND JIVE

Words and Music by
JOHNNY OTIS

WONDERFUL TONIGHT

Words and Music by
ERIC CLAPTON

It's late in the eve - ning;
We go to a par - ty,
It's time to go home __ now,

she's won - d'ring what clothes __ to wear. __
and ev - 'ry - one turns __ to see __
and I've got an ach - ing head. __

She puts on her make-
this beau - ti - ful la-
So I give her the car __

D. S. 𝄋 al Coda ⊕

Coda ⊕

Oh, my dar - ling, you are

won - der - ful ___ to - night." ___

rit.